W9-CKJ-062

Table of Contents

Crust gift-wraps a dish and makes it special — whether it's a pie for four-and-twenty blackbirds, or an hors d'oeuvre no bigger than an emerald.

With the world becoming ever smaller, our tastes are becoming increasingly international. For well-travelled tastes, we offer a world of crusty delights from Greek Spinach Rolls and French Apple Flan to Scallops San Tropez and Russian Piroshki. You'll also find an elegant version of the venerable Chicken Pie and a whole chapter devoted to quiche, the culinary French triumph. There are more ways than a baker's dozen of shaping pastry to your own ends. Crust enhances meat, vegetables, and desserts alike.

We preface this book with a repertory of basic crusts. None are difficult but all require a little endeavor. Also included are tips for quick pastry from mixes for the busy cook who needs a short-cut.

Recipes in this book are for six people.

BASIC CRUSTS

You don't have to have a white thumb to turn out good pastry. All it takes is a head for figures. If you know the difference between 5 Tbsp of cold water and 6 Tbsp of cold water, you'll turn out delectable crust with relative ease.

The following pastries are most frequently used for cooking in crust. First is the old fashioned, honest-to-goodness pie crust mother used to make before she succumbed to pie crust mix.

Pie Crust Pastry

All ingredients, as well as utensils, should be chilled in order that shortening can be quickly worked into flour without melting. Dough should be handled as little as possible, as over-mixing and handling tends to toughen pastry.

This recipe makes two 9-inch crusts:

> **2 1/4 cups sifted all-purpose flour**
> **3/4 cup cold vegetable shortening**
> **1 tsp salt**
> **5 Tbsp ice water**

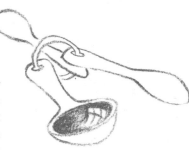

Cut the shortening into flour with a pastry blender, or two knives, until mixture is like coarse cornmeal. Dissolve salt in ice water. Add water a little at a time, mixing it lightly into the flour. Add only enough water to moisten flour so that dough will cling together. Wrap dough in wax paper and chill in refrigerator 1/2 hour.

6 Turn dough out on lightly floured board. Divide pastry in half and shape into 2 balls. Lightly flatten balls with a rolling pin into circles 1/2-inch thick. Roll out dough from center of each circle in all directions to make 2 circles 1/8-inch thick and 1 1/2-inches larger than inverted pie pan. Drape pastry circle over rolling pin so it may be easily transferred to pie plate. Fit pastry into bottom of pie plate without stretching the dough. Pat out all air pockets.

When filling has been poured in pie shell, place top circle of pastry over pie, turn under edges and flute edges of dough with a fork or pastry crimper. Pierce top of crust several places to let steam escape during baking.

Sweet Pie Crust Pastry (Pate Sucrée)

1 cup sifted all-purpose flour
2 oz butter
4 Tbsp sifted confectioners' sugar
2 egg yolks
Few drops vanilla

Here's a sweet version of pie crust for dessert pies, tarts, or flans.

Heap flour on a pastry board. Make a well in the center, and add butter, confectioners' sugar, egg yolks and a few drops of vanilla.

Using your finger tips, work ingredients into a smooth paste. Gradually work flour into the paste until dough is smooth. Form dough into a ball and wrap in wax paper. Refrigerate 1/2 hour before using.

Makes a 9-inch single pie crust, or flan shell, or six tarts.

Puff Pastry (Pâté Feuilletée)

It's not surprising that anything as sublime as puff pastry is time-consuming to make. That's part of its mystique. However, once you've mastered this leafy pastry, you'll delight in its many uses—especially as an elegant crust for meat pies or pastry shells.

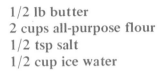

1/2 lb butter
2 cups all-purpose flour
1/2 tsp salt
1/2 cup ice water

It is important to make puff pastry under cool working conditions. Utensils and ingredients should be chilled —and cool your hands in cold water.

Knead butter until it is soft, and all water is removed. Keep in refrigerator.

Sift flour and salt in a mixing bowl; add water, working mixture just long enough to form a ball. Refrigerate dough for 20 minutes. (One of the secrets of making puff pastry is to keep the dough and the butter the same consistency.)

Place dough on a well-floured board, and roll into a rectangle 1/2-inch thick. Shape butter into a square 1/2-inch thick. Place butter in the center of dough and fold over both ends of the rectangle over the butter. Press ends together with a rolling pin. Wrap dough in wax paper and refrigerate 20 minutes.

Roll out dough on a floured board into a rectangle 15-inches long and 8-inches wide and 1/2-inch thick. Be sure that you lightly roll out the dough from the center to the edges, but never over the edges. It is essential that the butter does not break through the dough. Fold dough over into thirds as before. Roll out dough again into a rectangle, fold into thirds and refrigerate 20 minutes. This process is called a "turn" when the dough is rolled out, folded two times, and then chilled for 20 minutes.

Repeat two more "turns." After the final "turn" leave dough in the refrigerator 1 or 2 hours before cutting. Puff pastry must be ice cold when placed in a very hot oven.

Cream Puff Pastry (Chou Paste)

This versatile pastry shapes up everything from tiny hors d'oeuvres casings, to cream puff shells for desserts, or creamed entrees. It also makes a tasty topping for pastry-wrapped meats.

1 cup cold water
1/4 lb butter
1/2 tsp salt
1 cup sifted all-purpose flour
4 large eggs

Combine water, butter, and salt in a saucepan; bring to a boil and stir. Pour in flour all at once; remove pan from stove, and vigorously stir until mixture forms into a compact ball. Return to heat and beat mixture for exactly 1 minute.

Remove from stove and let cool for a few minutes. Beat in eggs, one at a time. Beat a few minutes after adding each egg until eggs are completely absorbed and batter is smooth.

Leave dough in a cool place 1 hour before using. Makes 2 1/2 cups of pastry.

Cream Puffs

Pipe pastry into 2-inch or 2 1/2-inch rounds on a lightly-greased baking sheet using a pastry bag and a large plain tube. Or, you can achieve the same results using 1 rounded Tbsp of pastry for each puff. Place cream puffs 2-inches apart on sheet.

Bake in a preheated 425 degree oven for 30 to 35 minutes until shells are golden brown. Do not underbake.

Turn off heat. Prick puffs with a knife to allow steam to escape. Leave puffs in oven for 20 minutes to allow centers to dry out.

•Cool. Split shells and fill with desired fillings. Makes 15 large cream puffs.

For small cream puffs, pipe pastry into 1-inch rounds; or drop pastry onto greased baking sheet using 1/2 tsp for each puff.

BASIC PIE SHELLS

A pie by any other name is a flan, a quiche or a tartlet. While these continental pies are baked in different pans, the following rules apply for preparing any baked, or partially baked, pie shell:

PARTIALLY BAKED PIE SHELL

Fit dough into pie pan and prick bottom of shell in several places with the tip of a sharp knife. Line pie shell with foil paper, and fill with beans or rice to keep pastry from rising or buckling during cooking. Place pie pan in the middle level of a preheated 400 degree oven for 8 minutes until pastry is set. Remove foil and beans or rice; prick shell again and bake another 2 or 3 minutes until pastry is firm but barely browned.

BAKED PIE SHELL

For a fully cooked pie shell, follow directions above but increase final baking time 8 to 10 minutes more until crust is lightly browned.

QUICHE SHELL

This savory custard pie requires a partially baked shell before the filling is added so the bottom crust stays crisp. Bake it in a traditional porcelain quiche dish, or a fluted tin quiche pan with a removable bottom, so the pie may be served separately.

FLAN RING

Flans are large tarts containing sweet or savory fillings. The flan shell is baked in a bottomless ring form which is placed on a greased, heavy baking sheet. Cut pastry large enough to overlap flan ring and firmly mold dough around the inside of ring. Roll rolling pin over top of rim to cut off excess dough. With your thumbs, push dough 1/8-inch above edge of ring to make an even, rounded rim on top. Make a decorative edge with a fork. The flan shell is partially baked or fully baked the same method as for a regular pie shell.

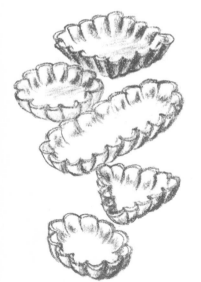

TARTLETS

A tartlet is a tiny tart—what else?—that holds a zesty filling as an hors d'oeuvre or a sublime sweet as a dessert. These miniature tarts are baked in round or oval tartlet tins approximately 2 to 4 inches in length. Prepare the shells the same way as for baked pie shells, but place the tartlet tins on a cookie sheet, and bake in a preheated 375 degree oven. Cool tartlets before removing from tins.

(Any of the culinary accessories mentioned in this book may be purchased at gourmet shops, department store, and some gift shops.)

The quickest way to a woman's heart—when it comes to cooking—is a short-cut. Ready-made mixes are a practical solution for the busy cook who can't make her own pastry. In some instances, such as filo pastry, which is the intricately made, paper-thin pastry used in Greek, Turkish, and Middle-Eastern delicacies, we recommend relying on the commercial product.

PIE CRUST MIX: Good for any recipe calling for regular pie crust. For quick Sweet Pie Crust Pastry, add 4 Tbsp of confectioners' sugar to pie crust mix.

FROZEN PUFF PASTRY SHELLS: Makes a surprisingly good substitute for puff pastry. Thaw shells and work dough into a ball. Roll out dough, and cut to desired shape. Refrigerate 1/2 hour before placing pastry in a hot oven.

FILO PASTRY: This delicate dough is sold in pastry sheets that are frozen. It must be thawed gradually. Leave pastry in refrigerator for four days, and finish thawing at average room temperature. Avoid using pastry when the humidity is very low or too high; it's best baked when the weather is temperate. Filo Pastry can also be used for any recipe calling for strudel dough. Available at Middle-Eastern markets and gourmet shops.

HOT ROLL MIX: A handy substitute for fresh yeast dough used in pizzas or Pissaladiere, the French pizza.

REFRIGERATED CRESCENT ROLLS: Great for making flaky turnovers or hors d'oeuvres wrappings. Shape dough into a ball, and roll out on a floured board. Cut to desired shape.

BISQUICK, CORN MUFFIN MIX: These mixes provide hearty toppings for single-crusted meat or chicken pies. Try them when you want a variation from regular pie crust.

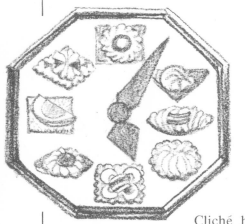

HORS D'OEUVRES TO MAKE YOU FAMOUS

Cliché hors d'oeuvres are like cliché conversations. They bore from within. A lively party thrives on imaginative, delectable canapés that taste as intriguing the umpteenth time around as on the first bite.

We give you a trayful of hot, crusty morsels to win you fame as a mini-chef. Bake these canapés in relays so you'll have a sizzling assortment waiting in the wings.

Pastry shells for hors d'oeuvres are made with pie crust, puff pastry, cream puff pastry, or miniature rolls. Tiny tartlet pans also shape up a variety of decorative appetizers.

2 1/2 cups flour
1/2 lb cream cheese
1/2 lb butter, softened
1/4 cup heavy cream
1/2 tsp salt
18 small pork sausages
1 cup white wine
1 cup water
Dijon mustard
1 egg yolk

Heap flour onto pastry board. Make a well in the center of the flour; and add the cream cheese, butter, cream, and salt. Work these ingredients into a paste with your fingertips gradually working in the flour. When the dough is smooth, wrap in wax paper and refrigerate for several hours.

Gently poach sausages in a skillet containing white wine and water. Simmer for 12 to 15 minutes, or until sausages are cooked. Drain sausages.

On a floured board roll out dough 1/4-inch thick and cut into small rectangles sufficiently large to encase each individual sausage. Brush rectangles with Dijon mustard and wrap around individual sausages sealing edges firmly. Brush dough with egg yolk mixed with 1 Tbsp of water; then prick with a fork.

Bake sausage rolls on a cookie sheet in a preheated 450 degree oven for 10 minutes; then reduce heat to 350 degrees and continue baking another 15 or 20 minutes—or until rolls are golden brown.

1/4 cup onion, grated
2 Tbsp butter
1/2 lb Swiss cheese, grated
3 eggs, beaten
1 1/2 cups heavy cream
1/4 tsp dry mustard
1 tsp salt
1/8 tsp cayenne pepper
1 recipe for pie crust pastry

Sauté onions in butter 5 minutes. Mix onions with cheese. In a bowl, stir together eggs, cream, dry mustard, salt and pepper. Combine egg mixture with cheese and onions.

Roll out pie crust pastry 1/8-inch thick on a floured board. Cut 24 rounds of dough to fit 2-inch tartlet tins; press dough into tins and pour in cheese filling.

Bake in a preheated 400 degree oven for 20 minutes, or until tarts are puffy and golden brown.

3 tsp butter
3 tsp flour
1/2 cup milk
1/4 tsp salt
1/8 tsp white pepper
1 Tbsp tomato sauce
4 hard-cooked eggs, diced
1/2 cup cooked mushrooms,
   drained and diced
1 Tbsp parsley, chopped
1 1/2 recipes for puff pastry or
   pie crust pastry
Egg yolk

Melt butter in a skillet, and stir in flour. Gradually add milk, and stir until white sauce thickens. Season with salt and white pepper. Add tomato sauce, eggs, mushrooms and parsley.

Roll out puff pastry, or pie crust pastry, 1/8-inch thick on a lightly-floured board. Cut into 2-inch circles with a fluted cookie cutter. Spoon 1 rounded tsp of mixture in the center of each round. Moisten edges of circles and cover with another round of dough. Press edges together firmly.

Place on cookie sheet. Brush with egg yolk mixed with 1 Tbsp of water. Prick top several places with the tip of a sharp knife.

Bake in a preheated (450 degree) oven for 12 to 15 minutes until crust is golden. Makes approximately 18 canapés.

Avocado Puffs

In a bowl combine avocado, lime juice, salt, Tabasco, garlic, onion, Worcestershire sauce, and cooked bacon. Mix well.

Pipe out cream puff pastry into 1-inch rounds on a greased cookie sheet using a pastry bag with a small plain tube. Or, drop 1/2 tsp of dough for each cream puff onto greased cookie sheet. Bake according to directions on page

Split shells and fill with avocado mixture. Makes approximately 18 to 24 canapés.

1 cup mashed avocado
1 Tbsp lime juice
1 tsp salt
Dash of Tabasco
1 clove garlic, finely minced
1 Tbsp onion, grated
1/2 tsp Worcestershire sauce
6 slices bacon, cooked and crumbled
1 recipe for cream puff pastry

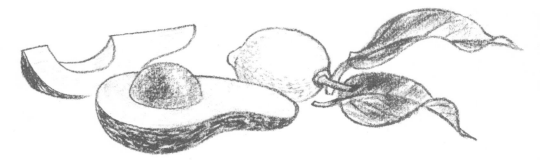

Greek Spinach Rolls

2 lbs fresh spinach
1/2 lb Mozzarella cheese, diced
1 cup Parmesan cheese, grated
4 Tbsp butter, diced
1/4 tsp pepper
1/4 tsp cinnamon
1/2 tsp salt
1/2 lb filo pastry
1 cup melted butter

Wash and dry spinach; remove stems. Chop spinach finely. Combine spinach with Mozzarella cheese, Parmesan, butter, pepper, cinnamon, and salt.

Use 2 sheets of filo pastry for each spinach roll. (See page 13 for preparation of filo pastry). Brush each sheet with melted butter and lay one on top of the other. (Keep remaining sheets covered with a damp cloth until ready to use.) Spoon out a band of spinach mixture lengthwise along one side of the sheet, leaving a margin of 2-inches on both ends. Turn in the ends and roll the sheet lengthwise into a long roll. Brush generously with melted butter. Continue making rolls in this manner until filling is used up.

Bake rolls on a greased baking sheet in a preheated 400 degree oven for 25 minutes, or until golden brown. Cut rolls diagonally into 2-inch pieces and serve hot. Makes about 40 rolls.

Oysters Ritz Bar

24 small oysters, shelled
2 Tbsp wine vinegar
6 Tbsp light olive oil
1/4 tsp salt
1/8 tsp ground black pepper
1/4 tsp powdered mustard
1 Tbsp parsley, chopped
1 recipe for pie crust pastry

Drain oysters. In a bowl combine wine vinegar, olive oil, salt, pepper, mustard, and parsley. Mix well. Marinate oysters in this French dressing for 3 hours in refrigerator.

Drain and dry oysters on paper towels.

Roll out pie crust dough on a floured board to 1/8-inch thickness. Cut into 2 1/2-inch rounds. Place 1 oyster on each round. Moisten edges, fold dough over, and seal edges together with a fork. Cut a small vent in each turnover.

Bake in a preheated 450 degree oven for 15 minutes, or until crust is golden.

1 cup ground cooked ham
1/3 cup sour cream
2 Tbsp mayonnaise
1 1/2 tsp curry powder
1/4 tsp salt
1/2 tsp powdered mustard
dash of cayenne pepper
2 Tbsp green onions, finely chopped
1 recipe for pie crust pastry, or
   puff pastry
Egg yolk

In a bowl combine ham, sour cream, mayonnaise, curry powder, salt, powdered mustard, cayenne pepper, and green onions. Blend well.

Roll out pie crust pastry or puff pastry 1/4-inch thick on a floured board. Cut into 3-inch rounds with a cutter. Place 1 rounded tsp of ham mixture on one side of round. Moisten edges of dough with water and fold over. Press edges together firmly. Prick top of turnovers with tip of a sharp knife. Brush pastry with egg yolk mixed with 1 Tbsp of water.

Place on cookie sheet and bake in a preheated 425 degree oven for 12 to 15 minutes until crust is golden brown. Makes approximately 18 to 24 turnovers.

1 recipe for pie crust pastry
2 Tbsp butter
2 Tbsp flour
1 cup light cream
2 Tbsp Parmesan cheese, grated
6 1/2-oz can crabmeat, boned and flaked

1/2 tsp salt
1/4 tsp pepper
1 egg yolk
2 Tbsp dry sherry

Garnish: Parmesan cheese

Roll out pie crust pastry 1/8-inch thick. Cut into small rounds to fit tartlet tins. Bake shells; cool. Remove tarts from tins.

Melt butter in skillet and add flour. Gradually stir in cream and cook until sauce thickens. Add cheese and stir until smooth. Add crabmeat, salt, and pepper. Remove from heat. Beat egg yolk with sherry and stir into creamed crab. Spoon mixture into baked tartlet shells and garnish with cheese.

Brown under a broiler for a few minutes. Makes approximately 18 to 24 tartlets.

Canapés da Napoli

1 cup Mozzarella cheese, finely chopped
1/4 cup parsley, finely chopped
1 cup prosciutto ham (or boiled ham),
   finely chopped
1/4 tsp freshly ground black pepper
1/4 tsp nutmeg
1/4 tsp oregano
3 doz miniature rolls
Butter

In a bowl, combine cheese, parsley, prosciutto ham (or boiled ham), pepper, nutmeg, and oregano.

Cut tops from miniature rolls; scoop out bread in the center, then butter. Spoon 1 Tbsp of filling into rolls and replace tops. Wrap rolls in foil and heat in the oven until cheese melts.

Makes approximately 3 dozen canapés.

1 1/2 recipes for pie crust pastry
1/2 cup Russian dressing
1/2 tsp dry mustard
6 1/2-oz can lobster, boned and flaked
1 10-oz can artichoke bottoms,
     drained and diced

Garnish: chopped parsley

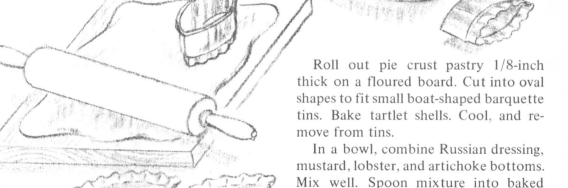

Roll out pie crust pastry 1/8-inch thick on a floured board. Cut into oval shapes to fit small boat-shaped barquette tins. Bake tartlet shells. Cool, and remove from tins.

In a bowl, combine Russian dressing, mustard, lobster, and artichoke bottoms. Mix well. Spoon mixture into baked barquette shells. Brown briefly under broiler and sprinkle with parsley. Makes approximately 3 dozen tarts.

QUICHE PIE — TEN WAYS

The French province of Lorraine gave the world its first interesting custard pie. Quiche Lorraine is a culinary triumph of Swiss cheese, onions and bacon baked in a rich custard. This grown-up tart serves as a first course for dinner, entree for lunch or hors d'oeuvres when sliced in thin wedges.

Happily, there are many variations of quiche—some are combined with seafood, others with vegetables, meat or zesty cheeses.

The following quiches are collectors' items. While they all share a custard base, each has a distinctive flavor and flair all its own.

1 1/2 cups cooked crabmeat or lobster
2 Tbsp green onions
1 Tbsp butter
2 Tbsp parsley, chopped
salt & pepper to taste
2 Tbsp dry vermouth
9-inch partially baked pie crust shell
4 eggs, lightly beaten
2 cups cream
1/8 tsp cayenne
1/4 tsp paprika

Remove shell bits from crabmeat or lobster and flake. Sauté onions in butter until tender. Combine onions with crab or lobster, parsley, salt & pepper to taste, and vermouth. Sprinkle crabmeat (or lobster) mixture over bottom of pie shell.

Combine eggs, cream, and cayenne; and pour over seafood.

Bake 15 minutes in a preheated 425 degree oven. Reduce temperature to 350 degrees and bake another 15 minutes.

1 Tbsp butter
2 Tbsp green onions, finely chopped
1 Tbsp flour
1 cup milk
6 eggs, lightly beaten
2 cups heavy cream
salt & pepper to taste
12 small link sausages
10-inch partially baked pie crust shell

Melt butter and sauté onions until tender. Stir in flour and pour in milk gradually. Simmer sauce for 15 minutes, stirring frequently. Remove from stove and cool slightly.

Beat eggs and heavy cream together, and gradually add to onion-milk sauce. Season with salt & pepper.

Cook sausages for 12 to 15 minutes according to directions on package. Drain. Place sausages on the bottom of pie shell like the spokes of a wheel. Strain the egg and cream mixture over the sausages.

Bake in a preheated 425 degree oven for 15 minutes. Reduce oven to 350 and bake another 15 minutes, or until custard is set.

Quiche Maison

2 Tbsp butter
6 green onions, finely chopped
1 lb ground sirloin
1 large tomato, peeled and chopped
1 tsp salt
1/2 tsp ground black pepper
1/2 tsp marjoram
1/4 tsp thyme
1 1/4 cups heavy cream
4 eggs, beaten
9-inch partially baked pie crust shell

Garnish: chopped parsley

Melt butter and sauté green onions and chopped sirloin until meat is lightly browned. Crumble meat with a fork as you cook it. Add tomato, salt, pepper, marjoram and thyme and simmer for 3 minutes. Cool.

Beat eggs and cream together and stir into meat-tomato mixture. Pour into pie shell.

Bake in a preheated 375 degree oven for 30 minutes. Garnish with chopped parsley.

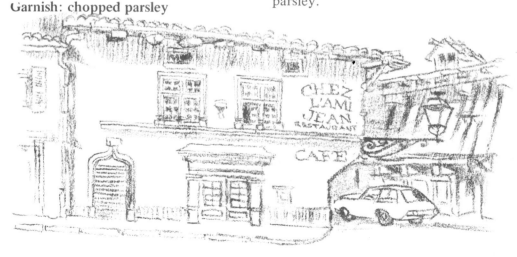

6 slices bacon cut into 1" lengths
1 cup onions, thinly sliced
1 1/2 cups Swiss cheese or
  Gruyere, diced
9-inch partially baked pie crust shell

4 eggs, beaten
2 cups cream
1/2 tsp salt
1/4 tsp ground nutmeg
1/4 tsp white pepper

Cook bacon until almost crisp. Remove bacon and drain on paper towel. Sauté onion in 2 Tbsp bacon drippings until tender. Cover bottom of partially baked pie shell with onions, bacon, and cheese.

Beat eggs and cream together with salt, nutmeg, and white pepper. Pour into pie shell.

Bake in a preheated 450 degree oven for 10 minutes; lower temperature to 350 degrees, and continue baking another 15 minutes.

2 Tbsp butter
2 Tbsp green onions, minced
2 packages frozen chopped
   spinach, thawed
1/2 tsp salt
1/4 tsp black pepper
1/4 tsp nutmeg
3/4 cup freshly grated Parmesan cheese
1 1/4 cups heavy cream
4 eggs, lightly beaten
9-inch partially baked pie crust shell

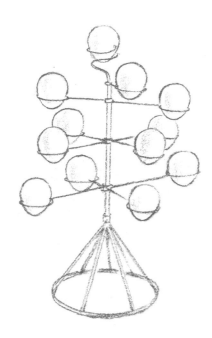

Melt butter and sauté onions until tender.

Cook spinach in a saucepan according to directions on the package. Drain spinach in a colander and press out all excess water. In a bowl combine spinach, onions, salt, pepper, nutmeg, and 1/2 cup cheese.

Beat cream and eggs together, and combine with spinach mixture.

Pour into pie shell, and sprinkle with remaining cheese. Bake in a 375 degree oven for 30 minutes.

3-oz Roquefort cheese or blue cheese
9-inch partially baked pie crust shell
5 eggs, lightly beaten
2 cups cream
1/4 cup sour cream
1/2 tsp salt
1/4 tsp pepper
1/4 tsp nutmeg

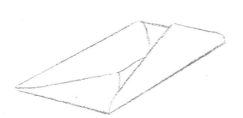

Crumble cheese and sprinkle on the bottom of pie shell.

Combine eggs with cream, sour cream, salt, pepper, and nutmeg. Pour through a strainer, and pour into pie shell.

Bake quiche 15 minutes at 425 degrees, then reduce heat to 350, and bake another 15 minutes until custard is set.

3/4 lb cooked shrimp, shelled and
   deveined
2 Tbsp parsley, chopped
1/4 cup dry sherry
1/4 cup cooked sliced mushrooms
9-inch partially baked pie crust shell
4 eggs, lightly beaten
1 3/4 cup cream
1/4 tsp nutmeg
1/2 tsp salt
1/4 tsp white pepper

Combine shrimp, parsley, and sherry in a bowl and marinate in refrigerator 1 hour. Stir in mushrooms.

Beat eggs and cream together and season with nutmeg, salt and pepper. Stir in shrimp-mushroom mixture, and pour into pie shell.

Bake in a preheated 425 degree oven for 15 minutes. Reduce temperature to 350 and bake another 15 minutes.

4 slices bacon
1 cup sliced leeks (white part only)
9-inch partially baked pie crust shell
4 eggs, lightly beaten
2 cups cream
1 Tbsp butter, melted
1 Tbsp flour
1/2 tsp salt
1/4 tsp dry mustard
1/8 tsp cayenne

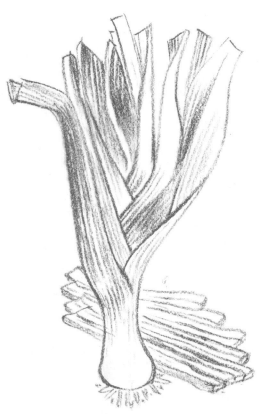

Cook bacon until crisp and crumble. Pour out all but 2 Tbsp of bacon drippings from skillet. Saute leeks in bacon drippings until tender. Combine leeks and bacon and spoon over the bottom of pie shell.

Stir eggs and cream together and add butter, flour, salt, dry mustard, and cayenne. Pour into pie shell.

Bake in a 375 degree oven for 30 minutes.

1 1/2 cups Cheddar cheese, diced
4-oz package smoked beef, shredded
9-inch partially baked pie crust shell
4 eggs, lightly beaten
1 Tbsp flour
2 cups cream
1/2 tsp salt
1/8 tsp cayenne
1/2 tsp dry mustard
1/8 tsp ground mace
1 Tbsp butter, melted

Sprinkle cheese and beef on the bottom of pie shell.

In a bowl mix together eggs, flour, cream, salt, cayenne, dry mustard, mace, and butter. Pour into pie shell.

Bake in a preheated 375 degree oven for 30 minutes.

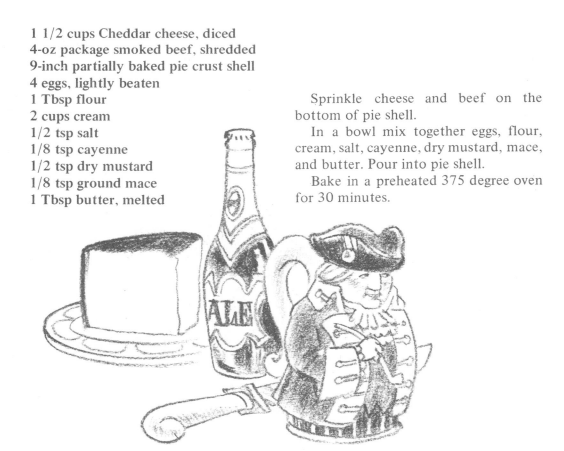

1/2 lb lean pork, finely diced
1/3 lb veal, finely diced
1 cup dry white wine
1 shallot, chopped
1 Tbsp parsley, chopped
1 clove garlic, finely chopped
2 Tbsp butter
1/2 tsp salt
1/4 tsp pepper
1 Tbsp parsley, finely chopped
9-inch partially baked pie crust shell
4 eggs, beaten
2 cups cream

Put pork and veal in a bowl with white wine, shallots, parsley, and garlic. Stir, then marinate meat in refrigerator overnight.

Drain and dry meat. Season with salt and pepper. Melt butter in a skillet and sauté meat for 10 minutes, stirring frequently. Remove meat from pan with slotted spoon and spread meat over the bottom of pie shell. Sprinkle with parsley. Cool.

Stir eggs and cream together and pour over meat.

Bake in a preheated 375 degree oven for 30 minutes.

PASTRY-WRAPPED ROASTS

A roast dressed in French pastry is elegant enough to go to a ball—or grace a dinner party.

The pastry-wrapped roast is a culinary art executed with the finesse of a couturier. Pastry is molded, trimmed, and tucked to cover the meat as decoratively as possible. As a finishing touch, pastry cut-outs are applied in a variety of designs—from flowers to crescent moons.

Several of these meats are adorned with a crisp, airy topping of cream puff pastry, or chou paste, which produces impressive results with little work.

3 to 4 lb leg-of-lamb, boned
2 Tbsp butter
2 lamb kidneys, cubed
2 Tbsp sherry wine
1 cup fresh mushrooms, sliced
1/2 tsp thyme
1/2 tsp rosemary
1/2 tsp tarragon
3 Tbsp butter, softened
1 tsp salt
1/2 tsp pepper
1 1/2 recipes for pie crust pastry
Egg yolk, beaten

Have butcher bone the shank end of a small leg-of-lamb leaving a pocket for stuffing.

Melt butter and saute lamb kidneys 1 minute. Add wine, mushrooms, thyme, rosemary, and tarragon. Sauté another 2 minutes. Spoon mixture into lamb pocket. Stitch opening closed with heavy thread. Mold lamb into compact shape. Rub with butter, salt and pepper. Roast meat in a preheated 400 degree oven for 35 minutes. Remove from oven and cool meat 15 minutes.

Roll out pie crust pastry 1/4-inch thick, and of sufficient size to cover lamb. Wrap lamb in dough. Trim edges of pastry, fold over corners; moisten edges with water and pinch pastry together so it is sealed. Make pastry cut-outs, moisten with water and decorate crust as desired. Brush pastry with egg yolk mixed with 1 Tbsp of water, and prick with fork several times.

Roast lamb in a 400 degree oven for 40 minutes until crust is golden brown.

Almond Pork Tenderloin 38

3 whole pork tenderloins
1 cup teriyaki sauce
1/2 cup dry sherry
toasted almond slivers
1/2 tsp salt
1/4 tsp pepper
1 tsp rosemary
2 1/4 cups cream puff pastry
  (chou paste)

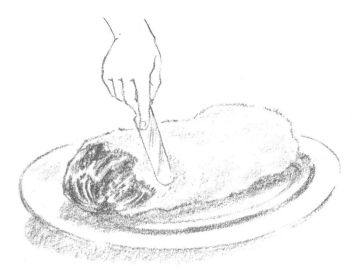

Marinate pork tenderloins in teriyaki sauce and sherry for 1 hour, turning frequently. Drain meat and insert almond slivers about 3/4-inch apart along top of tenderloins. Season with salt, pepper, and rosemary. Brown meat on all sides under a broiler for 10 minutes. Cool.

Prepare cream puff pastry. Place tenderloins on a baking dish, and spread top and sides (but not bottom) with a smooth layer of cream puff pastry—using about 3/4 of a cup per tenderloin. Score pastry lightly with a fork. Cover dish and refrigerate for 1/2 hour.

Bake in a 425 degree oven for 30 minutes, or until crust is golden brown. One tenderloin serves two or three people. Cut into individual servings at table.

4 lb filet of beef
1/4 lb butter, softened
1 tsp salt
1/2 tsp ground black pepper
1 onion, sliced
2 carrots, sliced
1/4 cup celery, sliced
1 1/2 recipes for puff pastry or
   pie crust pastry
3 oz pâté de foie gras
1 egg yolk
1 cup beef stock
1/4 cup fresh mushrooms, sliced
1 oz pâté de foie gras

Rub filet on all sides with butter and season with salt and pepper.

Spoon onion, carrots, and celery in the bottom of roasting pan. Place filet on top. Roast uncovered in a preheated 450 degree oven for 40 minutes—allowing 10 minutes to the lb. Cool.

Roll out puff pastry or pie crust pastry into a rectangle 1/4-inch thick. Pastry must be sufficiently wide to wrap around filet and overlap top 1-inch, and long enough to turn up 1-inch on both ends. Spread beef with pâté de foie gras on top and sides. Place meat in center of pastry rectangle and bring up both sides overlapping pastry 1-inch on top. Press seam together. Bring up both ends, moisten with water and press against meat to seal.

Place meat on baking sheet, seam side down. Decorate with strips of dough laid over top in lattice pattern. Brush crust with egg yolk mixed with 1 Tbsp water, and prick several places with a fork. Bake in a preheated 425 degree oven for 10 minutes; reduce to 350 degrees and bake another 20 minutes, or until crust is golden.

Pour beef stock into a pan with mushrooms and pate. Simmer 10 minutes. Serve sauce separately.

6 short loin lamb chops,
   cut 2-inches thick
3/4 cup dry sherry
1 tsp salt
1/2 tsp ground black pepper
1 tsp rosemary
1 garlic clove, minced
2 cups cream puff pastry (chou paste)

Remove all fat and gristle from chops. (With this dish it's important to invest in prime meat.) Marinate chops in sherry 1/2 hour before cooking.

Drain chops and season with salt, pepper, rosemary, and garlic. Brown chops under a broiler for 3 minutes on each side. Cool meat.

Prepare cream puff pastry and spread 1/3 cup of pastry over top and sides of each chop. Cover meat and chill in refrigerator 1/2 hour.

Bake chops in a preheated 425 degree oven for 30 minutes until pastry is puffed and golden brown.

6 chicken breasts, boned and skinned
4 Tbsp butter, melted
1 tsp salt
1/4 tsp pepper
Juice of 1/2 lemon
1 Tbsp parsley, chopped
Double recipe for puff pastry
6 thin slices baked ham
6 slices Swiss Cheese
1 egg yolk, beaten

Lay chicken breasts in shallow pan and brush with melted butter; season with salt, pepper, lemon juice, and parsley. Bake chicken in a preheated 375 degree oven for 15 minutes or until chicken is cooked. Reserve pan drippings. Cool chicken.

Roll out puff pastry 1/8-inch thick, and cut into six 6-inch squares. Place 1 slice of ham (cut the same size as chicken breast) on one half of each square. Top each slice of ham with 1 slice of Swiss Cheese, also cut the same size as chicken breast. Place 1 chicken breast over each slice of cheese and spoon over 1 Tbsp of pan drippings.

Individually fold half of each pastry square over chicken-ham-cheese filling, making a compact envelope. If necessary, cut away excess dough around edges. Moisten edges of dough and seal together by scoring with a fork. Cut several vents in top of crust and brush with egg yolk mixed with 1 Tbsp of water.

Bake turnovers in a preheated 450 degree oven for 10 minutes; reduce temperature to 350 and bake another 20 minutes, or until crust is golden.

6 to 7 lb ready-to-eat ham, shank end
1/2 cup sherry
1 cup orange juice
1/3 cup brown sugar
2 Tbsp Dijon prepared mustard
1/2 tsp black pepper
1/2 tsp cinnamon
1/2 tsp powdered cloves
1/3 tsp fine dry bread crumbs
4 tsp orange rind, grated
1 1/2 recipes for pie crust pastry
Egg yolk, beaten
1/4 cup sherry

Remove skin and excess fat from ham and place in a roasting pan. Combine sherry and orange juice, and pour over ham. Cover and bake in a 350 degree oven for 1 1/2 hours. Baste frequently. Remove ham and cool.

Combine brown sugar, mustard, pepper, cinnamon, and cloves; and spread over ham surface. Mix breadcrumbs and orange rind, and press into ham with a spatula so that crumbs adhere.

Roll out chilled pie crust pastry 1/4-inch thick of sufficient size to cover ham. Place meat on a baking sheet and cover top and sides, but not bottom, of ham with pastry. Mold dough to the ham with your hands, making as attractive a wrapping as possible. Make pastry cut-outs, moisten with water and place on top and sides of ham. Cut a 1/4-inch diameter hole in top center of crust. Brush dough with egg mixed with 1 Tbsp water.

Bake ham in a 350 degree oven for 40 minutes, or until crust is golden. Spoon sherry through hole in crust before serving.

2 1 1/2 lb veal filets
3 Tbsp butter, softened
1 tsp salt
1/4 tsp pepper
1 tsp rosemary
4 oz pâté de foie gras

3/4 cup fresh mushrooms, chopped
1 Tbsp butter
1 1/2 recipes for puff pastry, or
   pie crust pastry
Egg yolk
1 Tbsp milk

Rub veal filets with butter, and season with salt, pepper, and rosemary. Place in a pan and roast in a 400 degree oven for 15 minutes. Cool.

Spread top and sides of filets with pâté de foie gras. Sauté mushrooms in butter until tender. Drain mushrooms and spread them along top of filets.

Roll out chilled puff pastry, or pie crust pastry, 1/4-inch thick. Cut into two rectangles that are 1-inch longer than filets on both ends, and sufficiently wide to wrap around meat and overlap 1-inch on top. Place one filet in center of each rectangle; bring up sides of pastry over top of filets, overlapping 1-inch. Press seam together. Bring up

ends of dough and press against meat to seal the edges. Cut several small vents in the top of the crust. Decorate with pastry cut-outs. Brush crust with egg yolk mixed with milk.

Bake in a 400 degree oven for 45 minutes. If crust browns too quickly, cover with foil. One filet of veal will serve three people. Cut into individual servings at table.

DINNER IN A PIE

Meat pies are a legacy of the middle ages when men relished a hearty meal after a hard day of chivalry. While today's defenders-of-the-castle fight freeways instead of dragons, they still love pie for dinner.

Some pies are simple, others elegant; they're pies for budgets, and pies for upper-crust parties. Whatever the ingredients, they're all uniquely satisfying.

Many dinner pies are baked in deep pie tins, or baking dishes. When a pie is made with a double-crust, we suggest a spring-form pan, or a pan with a removable bottom so the pie may be unmolded and served separately.

6 halves of chicken breasts, boned
   and skinned
1 tsp salt
3 Tbsp butter
1 cup chicken broth
8 canned artichoke bottoms, quartered
2 Tbsp butter
3/4 cup dry white wine
2 Tbsp cornstarch
3 Tbsp sour cream
1/4 tsp nutmeg
salt & pepper to taste
Pie crust pastry for deep double-crust
   pie
4 oz boiled ham, cut in 1/2 inch strips
4 hard-cooked eggs, sliced
1 cup Swiss cheese, shredded
1 egg yolk, beaten

Season chicken breasts with salt, and sauté in butter until lightly browned. Pour in chicken stock; cover and simmer until chicken is tender in about 10 or 15 minutes. Reserve 1/2 cup of stock.

Cut chicken breasts into 1-inch lengths, 1/2-inch wide.

Sauté artichoke in butter for a few minutes. Heat 1/2 cup of chicken stock with wine, and thicken with cornstarch. Stir in sour cream, nutmeg, and season with salt & pepper to taste.

Prepare pie crust pastry for standard size pie increasing proportions by 1/3 more to allow for a deep pie pan. Use 2/3 of the pastry to line a 9-inch, 2 1/2-inch deep spring-form pan—or pan with removable bottom.

Spoon out chicken, artichoke, ham, and egg slices over bottom of shell. Pour over wine-chicken sauce, and top with cheese. Roll out remaining dough and cover top; pinch edges of top and bottom crust together to seal. Cut several small vents in top. Brush with egg yolk mixed with 1 Tbsp water.

Bake in a 425 degree oven for 15 minutes; reduce to 350 degrees, and bake another 20 minutes. Cool slightly before unmolding.

Roman Vitello and Sweetbread Pie   46

1 1/2 lbs thinly sliced veal cut in
   1-inch strips
1/2 tsp salt
1/4 tsp pepper
3 Tbsp butter
1 clove garlic, minced
1 cup white wine
1/2 lb fresh mushrooms, sliced
2 Tbsp butter
1 lb sweetbreads, poached
Pie crust pastry for a 10-inch
   double crust
2 Tbsp parsley, chopped
1/2 cup chicken stock
2 Tbsp cornstarch
3 Tbsp milk

Season veal with salt & pepper, and sauté in butter until lightly brown. Add garlic and wine. Cover and simmer 10 minutes. Remove veal and reserve stock.

Sauté mushrooms in butter until tender.

Remove membranes from cooked sweetbreads and cut into bite-size pieces.

Roll out pastry 1/8-inch thick. Line pie plate with half the pastry. Layer veal, sweetbreads, and mushrooms in alternate layers in pie shell, and sprinkle with parsley.

Combine veal-wine stock with chicken stock and bring to boil. Thicken with cornstarch blended with 2 Tbsp water. Pour over pie.

Cover pie with remaining pastry; turn under edges, and flute with a fork. Cut several vents in crust, and brush with milk.

Bake in a 400 degree oven for 40 minutes.

2 lbs round steak, cut into 1-inch cubes
3 veal kidneys
1/2 cup flour
6 Tbsp butter
1 tsp salt
1/4 tsp ground black pepper
2 onions, thinly sliced
2 cups beef stock
1 cup red wine
1/2 lb fresh mushrooms, sliced
1/2 tsp rosemary
1 Tbsp flour
Puff pastry, or pie crust pastry, for
    single crust
Egg yolk, beaten

Wash kidneys and remove membranes, fat, and tubes. Cut into quarters. Dredge steak and kidneys in flour. Quickly brown in butter, and season with salt and pepper. Add onions and cook until onions are soft, but not browned. Put meat and onions in a saucepan with beef stock, red wine, mushrooms, and rosemary. Cover and simmer for 1 1/2 hours, or until meat is tender. Stir in flour mixed with 1 Tbsp water to thicken gravy. Transfer contents to a deep baking dish.

Roll out puff pastry, or pie crust pastry. to 1/4-inch thickness. Cut dough to fit top of baking dish, and cover pie. Moisten edges of dough and seal against rim. Cut several vents in top of pie, and brush with egg yolk mixed with 1 Tbsp of water.

Bake in a 425 degree oven for 10 minutes; reduce temperature to 350 and bake another 20 minutes, or until crust is golden.

1 cup water
1/4 lb butter
1/4 tsp salt
1 cup flour
4 eggs, beaten
2 cups grated Swiss cheese or
    Gruyere cheese
5 Tbsp butter
5 Tbsp flour
2 1/2 cups milk
1 tsp salt
1/4 tsp ground white pepper
Pie pastry for 9-inch single-crust pie
2 Tbsp butter, melted

Pour water into a saucepan and add butter and salt. Heat until butter melts; add flour all at time, stirring constantly until mixture forms into a stiff ball. Remove from stove and beat eggs into dough gradually until eggs are absorbed and dough is smooth. Stir in 1 cup of cheese.

Shape dough into 1-inch balls and poach gently in salted, barely simmering water for 10 minutes, then drain. These little dumplings are called Gnocchi (rhymes with pokey).

Melt butter in a skillet, and stir in flour. Gradually add milk, and cook until sauce thickens. Season with salt and white pepper. Stir in 3/4 cup of cheese, and heat until cheese melts. Spoon Gnocchi into sauce.

Roll out pie crust pastry 1/8-inch thick, and line a 9-inch pie plate. Turn under edges of pastry and flute. Pour Gnocchi and sauce into pie shell. Sprinkle with remaining 1/4 cup of cheese, and spoon melted butter over top.

Bake pie in a preheated 450 degree oven for 10 minutes. Reduce heat to 350, and continue baking for 20 to 30 minutes longer until top of Gnocchi is golden brown.

4 Tbsp butter
4 Tbsp flour
1 cup chicken stock
1 cup cream
salt and pepper to taste
12 small mushroom caps
2 Tbsp butter
10 small cooked onions
2 cups cooked chicken, cut into
   1-inch pieces
1 Tbsp parsley, chopped
1/4 tsp paprika
Puff pastry or pie crust pastry
   for single crust
1 egg yolk, beaten

Melt butter and add flour. Gradually stir in chicken stock and cream and cook until sauce thickens. Season with salt and pepper to taste.

Sauté mushrooms in butter until tender. Add mushrooms, onions, and chicken to sauce. Sprinkle with parsley and paprika. Spoon into baking dish.

Roll out puff pastry or pie crust pastry 1/4-inch thick, and cut to desired size to fit top of dish. Cover with pastry; moisten edges and seal to dish. Use any excess dough to make a fluted border around inside rim of dish.

Brush pastry with egg yolk mixed with 1 Tbsp of water. Bake in a 425 degree oven for 10 minutes; reduce heat to 350 degrees, then bake another 20 minutes until crust is golden brown.

1 lb Italian sausage
1 lb ricotta cheese
4 eggs, beaten
1/2 cup Parmesan cheese, grated
1 cup Swiss cheese, shredded
1/4 cup parsley chopped
1/2 lb center-cut ham, cut in fine,
   short strips
Pie crust pastry for 10-inch
   double-crust pie
3 Tbsp milk

Cook sausage in oven for 30 minutes. Cool; remove skin and chop meat.

Beat ricotta cheese·and eggs together. Stir in Parmesan cheese, Swiss cheese, parsley, ham strips, and sausage. Blend well.

Roll out pie crust pastry 1/8-inch thick, and use half the pastry to line pie pan. Spoon in sausage-cheese filling. Roll out remaining dough, and fit over the top of pie. Turn under edges of pastry and flute. Cut several vents in crust, and brush with milk.

Bake in a 375 degree oven for 35 to 40 minutes until crust is golden.

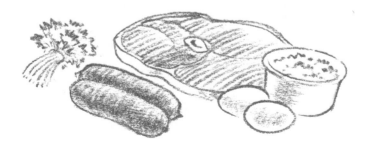

3/4 lb veal, cut into 1-inch pieces
3/4 lb lean pork, cut into 1-inch pieces
1/2 cup flour
4 Tbsp butter
1 tsp salt
1/2 tsp pepper
1/2 tsp paprika
3 cups beef stock
1 bay leaf

2 whole cloves
2 carrots, sliced
1/3 cup celery, diced
10 small white boiling onions, peeled
1 cup potatoes, cut in 1-inch cubes
1 Tbsp flour
Pie crust pastry, or puff pastry, for
   single crust
Egg yolk, beaten

Dredge meat in flour. Melt butter and quickly brown meat. Season with salt, pepper, and paprika. Pour in beef stock and add bay leaf and cloves. Cover and simmer 30 minutes.

Add carrots, celery, onions and potatoes. Simmer another 30 minutes.

Strain stock reserving 2 cups. Dissolve flour in 1 Tbsp water and stir into stock; simmer until gravy slightly thickens. Spoon meat and vegetables into baking dish and pour over gravy.

Roll out pie crust pastry, or puff pastry, 1/4-inch thick; and cut dough to desired size to fit top of dish. Cover with pastry, moisten edges of dough and seal to rim. Cut vents in top of crust, and brush with milk.

Bake in a preheated 425 degree oven for 10 minutes; reduce to 350, and bake another 20 minutes.

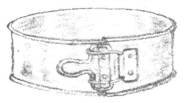

2 lbs boneless veal, cut into
   1-inch pieces
1 tsp salt
1/4 tsp pepper
Pie crust pastry for deep,
   double-crust pie
7 cups soft bread crumbs
1/2 cup flour
2 onions, minced
3 Tbsp parsley, chopped
1 lemon rind, grated
2 tsp salt
1/2 tsp pepper
1/2 tsp paprika
1/4 tsp nutmeg
1 1/3 cup white wine
1 egg yolk, beaten

Remove any fat or gristle from veal. Season with salt and pepper.

Prepare pie crust pastry for standard size pie, increasing proportions by 1/3 to allow for deep pie pan. Use 2/3 of the pastry to line a 9-inch, 2 1/2-inch deep spring-form pan, or pan with removable bottom.

Combine bread crumbs, flour, onions, parsley, lemon rind, salt, pepper, paprika, and nutmeg; and blend well. Spoon out a layer of this mixture over the bottom of pie pan. Cover with a layer of veal and press down. Repeat layers of bread crumbs and veal, pressing down ingredients each time, ending with bread crumbs on top. Pour wine over top.

Roll out remaining dough, and cover top of pie. Pinch edges of top and bottom crust together to seal. Decorate with pastry-cut outs. Cut several vents in top of crust, and brush with egg yolk mixed with 1 Tbsp of water.

Bake in a slow oven (300 degrees) for 3 hours. Cover crust with foil if it becomes too brown.

4 slices bacon, diced
1/4 cup green pepper, chopped
1/4 cup green onions, finely chopped
1 pint oysters, drained
1 cup flour
2 Tbsp parsley, chopped
2 Tbsp lemon juice
1/2 tsp salt
1/2 cup oyster liquor
1/2 cup white wine
Pie crust pastry for single crust

Fry bacon until crisp. Remove bacon and reserve 2 Tbsp of bacon drippings. Sauté green pepper and green onions in bacon fat until tender.

Gently roll oysters in flour, and place in a buttered rectangular pan. Spoon over green pepper, green onions, and bacon; season with parsley, lemon juice, and salt.

Combine oyster liquor from drained oysters with white wine. Pour over vegetables and oysters.

Roll out pie crust pastry 1/8-inch thick. Cut dough into strips 3/4-inch wide and lay over pie in a criss-cross lattice pattern. Bake in a preheated 425 degree oven for 15 minutes.

2 lbs sirloin steak
1/2 cup flour
3 Tbsp butter
1 tsp salt
1/2 tsp ground black pepper
3/4 cup green onions, finely sliced
2 cups fresh mushrooms, thinly sliced
2 Tbsp flour
1 cup beef stock
1/2 cup burgundy wine
Puff pastry, or pie crust pastry, for
    single crust
1 egg yolk, beaten

Cut steak into 1-inch squares, 1/2-inch thick. Dredge meat in flour, and lightly brown in butter. Season with salt and pepper. Transfer meat to a baking dish.

Mix green onions and mushrooms with flour, and spoon vegetables on top of meat.

Combine beef stock and wine and pour over onions and mushrooms.

Roll out puff pastry, or pie crust pastry, 1/4-inch thick; and cut top to fit baking dish. Cover dish; moisten edges of pastry and seal against rim. Cut several vents in crust, and brush with egg yolk mixed with 1 Tbsp water.

Bake pie in a preheated 425 degree oven for 10 minutes; reduce to 350 degrees, and bake another 20 minutes until crust is golden.

PARTY VEGETABLES

The difference between party vegetables and ordinary garden variety vegetables is imagination.

Party vegetables are flavored with a heady touch of wine, dressed in an exquisite sauce, or combined with other savory foods. When they're baked in a flaky pie crust, they make a stellar attraction for lunch—or a tasty complement to a simple steak or roast dinner.

Pie crust pastry for double-crust
6 ears of fresh corn, shucked
3 hard-cooked eggs, sliced
3 green onions, minced
2 Tbsp parsley, finely chopped
1 Tbsp flour
1 Tbsp sugar
1 1/2 tsp salt
1/4 tsp pepper
4 Tbsp butter
3/4 cup cream

Roll out pie crust pastry 1/8-inch thick. Use half the dough to line a 9-inch pie plate.

Cut corn from cob with a sharp knife, making 3 1/2 cups of corn kernels. Layer corn, eggs, onions and parsley into pie shell.

Combine flour, sugar, salt & pepper, and sprinkle over corn. Dot with butter and pour cream over top.

Roll out remaining pie crust and place over the top of pie. Turn under edges of pastry and flute. Cut several vents in crust, and brush with milk.

Bake for 10 minutes at 400 degrees. Reduce heat to 350 degrees and bake another 45 minutes. If crust becomes too brown, cover with foil.

2 lbs small, fresh mushrooms
4 Tbsp butter
1/2 tsp salt
1/4 tsp pepper
Juice of 1/2 lemon
2 Tbsp butter
4 Tbsp flour
1 1/2 cups chicken stock
1/4 cup sherry
1/2 cup heavy cream, scalded
salt and pepper to taste
1 Tbsp parsley, chopped
Pie crust pastry or puff pastry for single
    crust
Egg yolk, beaten

Wash and dry mushrooms and trim off stems.

Melt butter in a skillet and add mushrooms, seasoning with salt, pepper and lemon juice. Sauté 10 minutes, stirring frequently. Spoon mushrooms into a buttered baking dish. Add 2 more Tbsp of butter to juices in skillet and stir in flour. Gradually stir in chicken stock and cook until sauce thickens. Add sherry and heavy cream and salt & pepper to taste. Pour sauce over mushrooms and sprinkle with parsley.

Roll out pie crust pastry or puff pastry 1/4-inch thick and cut pastry to fit top of baking dish. Cover dish with pastry, moisten edges and seal to rim. Brush crust with egg yolk mixed with 1 Tbsp water and prick top several places with a fork.

Bake in a preheated 425 degree oven for 10 minutes, reduce to 350 degrees and bake another 20 minutes.

3 large sweet potatoes
2 egg yolks, beaten
1/4 tsp nutmeg
1/4 tsp salt
2 Tbsp brown sugar
Pie crust pastry for single crust
2 egg whites
2 Tbsp powdered sugar

Boil sweet potatoes until tender. Peel and mash. Beat in egg yolks, nutmeg, salt, and brown sugar, then stir until potatoes are creamy.

Roll out pie crust pastry 1/8-inch thick and line a 9-inch pie pan.

Spoon sweet potatoes into pastry shell and bake in a 400 degree oven for 25 minutes until crust is golden. Cool.

Beat egg whites with sugar until they're stiff. Spread meringue over top of pie, and bake in a 300 degree oven until meringue is lightly browned. Serve hot.

2 cups milk
1 bay leaf
1/2 onion, sliced
4 sprigs parsley
1/2 tsp peppercorns
1 lb asparagus
4 Tbsp butter
1/3 cup ham, diced
3 Tbsp flour
1 tsp salt
9-inch baked pie shell
1/4 cup Parmesan cheese, grated
3/4 cup dry bread crumbs
1/2 tsp paprika
2 Tbsp butter

Heat milk in a saucepan and add bay leaf, onion, parsley and peppercorns. Bring to a simmer; remove from heat, and let stand 1 hour. Strain milk.

Cut off tough ends of asparagus; wash thoroughly and simmer in boiling, salted water for 10 minutes or until asparagus is tender. Drain.

Melt butter and saute ham until lightly browned. Sprinkle in flour and stir. Gradually add seasoned milk, and stir until sauce thickens. Season with salt.

Arrange half the asparagus on the bottom of baked pie shell with tips toward the center like spokes. Cover asparagus with the ham-white sauce. Arrange 1/2 of remaining asparagus with tips turned outward toward rim of pie; cover with remaining sauce. Place the rest of the asparagus with tips toward center of pie. Sprinkle with cheese combined with bread crumbs, and garnish with paprika. Dot with butter.

Bake in a 400 degree oven for 10 minutes until top has browned.

9-inch partially baked flan ring
2 Tbsp olive oil
2 onions, finely chopped
1 clove garlic, minced
6 large tomatoes, peeled and sliced
1 zucchini, thinly sliced

3 Tbsp parsley, finely chopped
1/2 tsp basil
1 tsp salt
1/4 tsp ground black pepper
2 eggs, well beaten
1/4 cup Parmesan cheese, grated

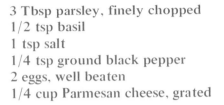

Bake flan according to directions on page 11 using pie crust pastry.

Heat olive oil in a skillet and sauté onions and garlic until lightly browned. Add tomatoes, zucchini, parsley, basil, salt and pepper. Simmer until vegetables are tender in about 15 minutes. Pour vegetables into the partially baked flan ring. Pour eggs over the top and sprinkle with Parmesan cheese.

Bake in a 400 degree oven for 15 minutes or until crust is golden brown. Remove flan ring before serving. (This dish may also be made in a regular 9-inch pie plate.)

SAVORY FILLINGS FOR SHELLS

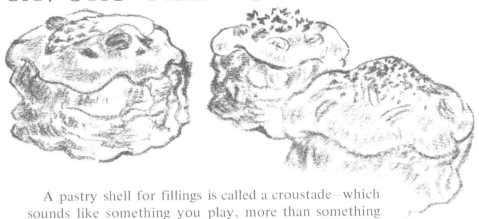

A pastry shell for fillings is called a croustade—which sounds like something you play, more than something you eat. By any name, these airy casings hold versatile fillings for luncheon and supper dishes.

Aside from the bouchee puff pastry shells most commonly used for creamed fillings, there are a number of tasty casings you can make from pie crust pastry, cream puff shells or even Junior's sandwich bread—as you'll see on the following pages.

Serve one or two croustades per serving, depending on appetites.

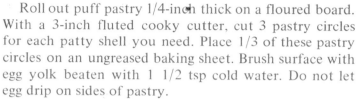

Roll out puff pastry 1/4-inch thick on a floured board. With a 3-inch fluted cooky cutter, cut 3 pastry circles for each patty shell you need. Place 1/3 of these pastry circles on an ungreased baking sheet. Brush surface with egg yolk beaten with 1 1/2 tsp cold water. Do not let egg drip on sides of pastry.

Cut out the centers of the next 1/3 of the pastry circles with a 2-inch cooky cutter, making a ring. Place one ring on each of the pastry circles on the baking sheet. Brush with egg yolk.

Press a 1 1/2-inch cooky cutter into the centers of the remaining 1/3 pastry circles, but do not cut through the dough. Place these circles on top of the rings of pastry. Brush again with egg yolk. Chill pastry shells 1/2 hour.

Bake shells in a preheated 450 degree oven for 10 minutes. Reduce heat to 350 degrees, and bake for 20 minutes longer until shells are golden.

Remove the indented centers of top layer with a pointed knife. Return shells to oven and bake another 5 or 10 minutes longer until interior of shells are firm and dry.

Pie Crust Croustades

Croustades of pie crust pastry are easily fashioned in almost any shape or size desired. Simply mold pastry, that has been rolled out 1/4-inch thick, over any inverted pan that is oven proof—such as muffin or custard cups, pie plate, ring molds, etc. Pan must be buttered and dough should be pressed snugly onto the bottom and sides of pan.

To prevent pastry from puffing during baking, lightly prick dough with a fork at frequent intervals on the sides and bottom of the shell.

Refrigerate pastry for one hour before baking.

Bake in a preheated 425 degree oven for 12 to 15 minutes until shell is lightly browned. Cool 5 minutes before unmolding shell from pan and place on a rack.

Bread Croustades

Slice crust from a loaf of day-old unsliced white sandwich bread. Cut 3-inch slices of bread for each bread case you need. Hollow out inside of bread with a small knife leaving a 1/4-inch shell on the sides and bottom like an open-topped box. Tap down bread on the inside with your fingertips.

Brush inside and outside, but not underside, of croustade with melted butter.

Toast for 5 to 10 minutes in oven until croustade is lightly browned. Spoon in filling.

1/4 cup onions, finely chopped
1/4 cup apple, peeled, cored and finely
  chopped
4 Tbsp butter
4 Tbsp flour
1 cup chicken broth
1 cup cream

2 tsp curry powder
salt & pepper to taste
3 cups cooked chicken, diced
3 Tbsp raisins
6 pastry or bread shells

Garnish: chutney

Saute onions and apple in butter until very tender. Stir in flour and blend well. Gradually add chicken broth and cream, then stir until sauce thickens. Season with curry powder, and salt & pepper to taste.

Add chicken and raisins, then heat. Spoon into pastry, or bread shells, and top each shell with 1 Tbsp of chutney.

1 cup mayonnaise
1/4 tsp anchovy paste
1 hard-cooked egg white, finely chopped
1 Tbsp lemon juice
1/4 cup dry white wine
2 Tbsp parsley, finely chopped
2 Tbsp fresh chervil, chopped
2 Tbsp capers
2 Tbsp green onions, chopped
2 Tbsp shallots, peeled and chopped
3 cups medium-sized cooked shrimp,
    peeled and deveined
6 pastry or bread shells
1 tsp paprika

Combine mayonnaise, anchovy paste, egg white, and lemon juice; and blend well.

Pour wine into a saucepan and add parsley, chervil, capers, onions, and shallots. Simmer until all but 1 Tbsp of liquid remains. Cool, and blend seasonings with mayonnaise, Stir in shrimp.

Spoon into pastry or bread shells and garnish with paprika.

3 pairs veal sweetbreads
1 tsp salt
2 Tbsp lemon juice
2 ribs celery
1/4 cup onions, chopped
1 tsp salt
4 Tbsp butter
4 Tbsp flour
2 cups sweetbreads stock
1 cup half-and-half
salt & pepper to taste
1 cup cooked ham, diced
6 pastry or bread shells

Garnish: chopped parsley

Soak sweetbreads in water with 1 tsp salt for 15 minutes. Rinse and drain.

Simmer sweetbreads in a saucepan with water to cover, together with lemon juice, celery, onions, and salt. Poach for 20 minutes. Drain sweetbreads, reserve stock; cool them in cold water and remove membranes before cutting into 1/2-inch cubes.

Melt butter in a skillet and stir in flour. Gradually add sweetbread stock, and half-and-half, then stir until sauce thickens. Season with salt and pepper to taste. Add sweetbreads and ham, and heat.

Spoon into pastry or bread shells, and garnish with parsley.

1 dozen eggs
1 tsp salt
1/4 tsp pepper
3/4 lb small cooked shrimp, shelled and
    deveined
2 1/2-oz can cooked button mushrooms
3 Tbsp butter
6 pastry or bread shells

Garnish: chopped parsley

Beat eggs and season with salt and pepper. Add shrimp and drained mushrooms.

Melt butter in a skillet over a low flame. Pour in eggs and gently stir until eggs are cooked but still moist. Do not overcook.

Spoon into hot pastry or bread shells and garnish with parsley.

2 lbs scallops
1 cup white wine
1 cup water
1/2 lb fresh mushrooms, sliced
2 Tbsp butter
1 pint sour cream
Juice of 1/2 lemon
1/2 tsp salt
1/4 tsp ground black pepper
1/4 lb Swiss cheese, shredded
4 Tbsp butter
6 pastry or bread shells

Wash scallops, and poach in white wine & water for 10 minutes. Drain, and slice scallops into small pieces.

Saute mushrooms in butter until tender. Drain mushrooms.

In the top of a double boiler, combine sour cream, lemon juice, salt, black pepper, Swiss cheese, and butter. Slowly heat and stir until cheese melts. Do not let sauce boil. Add scallops and mushrooms, and briefly heat.

Spoon into pastry or bread shells.

4 Tbsp butter
4 Tbsp flour
1 cup chicken stock
1 cup cream
3 Tbsp sherry
salt & pepper to taste
1 cup ham, diced
1 cup cooked chicken, diced
1/2 cup canned button mushrooms,
   drained
6 pastry or bread shells

Garnish: canned white asparagus tips

   Melt butter and stir in flour. Gradually add chicken stock and cream; and stir until sauce thickens. Season with sherry and salt & pepper. Add ham, chicken, and mushrooms.

   Spoon into pastry or bread shells. Garnish with white asparagus tips.

1/4 cup green onions, chopped
1/4 cup green pepper, chopped
4 Tbsp butter
2 Tbsp flour
1 1/2 cups milk
1/2 cup Cheddar cheese, shredded
1 tsp salt
1/4 tsp pepper
1 tsp dry mustard
3 dashes Tabasco
2 6 1/2-oz cans crabmeat, boned
    and flaked
6 pastry or bread shells

Garnish: paprika

Sauté green onions and green pepper in 2 Tbsp of butter until tender.

Melt 2 Tbsp of butter in a double boiler and stir in flour. Gradually add milk and cook until sauce thickens. Add cheese, and stir until cheese melts. Season with salt, pepper, mustard, and Tabasco. Add crabmeat, green onions, and green pepper, then heat.

Spoon into pastry or bread shells and garnish with paprika.

COOKING IN CRUST
AROUND THE WORLD

Pastry is as universal as love—and twice as substantial. Every country has its crusty specialties which are traditionally part of its cuisine. They vary from the robust Cornish Pasties of England to the exotic delicacies of Greece and Turkey.

These international foods are savored as a casual snack or small feast any time of day. Piroshki, for example, is a Russian meat or vegetable turnover traditionally served with soup, but it also makes a great breakfast when you're hungry as a Russian bear. Chicken Pâté en Croûte slices into an elegant first course for dinner—or packs up for a picnic lunch in the singing wilderness.

Turkish Lamb Rolls

2 small onions, finely chopped
2 Tbsp olive oil
1 1/2 lb ground lamb
2 Tbsp tomato paste
1 1/2 tsp salt
1/4 tsp ground black pepper
1 clove garlic, minced
1/4 tsp thyme
2 eggs, beaten
1/2 cup pistachio nuts, shelled
   and chopped
16 sheets of filo pastry
1/2 cup butter, melted

Saute onions in olive oil until tender. Add lamb and brown, crumbling meat with a fork. Season meat and onions with tomato paste, salt, pepper, garlic, and thyme. Remove pan from stove and cool meat slightly. Stir in eggs and nuts and blend well.

Lay out 1 sheet of filo pastry. (Keep remaining pastry covered with a damp towel.) Brush pastry with butter, and fold in half making a rectangle. Brush pastry again and spoon 1/3 cup of meat mixture along one end of rectangle leaving a margin of 1 1/2-inches on both sides. Fold in sides and roll up pastry. Brush with butter and place on a greased baking sheet. Repeat process until filling is used up; this recipe makes about 16 rolls.

Bake in a preheated 400 degree oven for 20 minutes, or until crust is golden brown.

Italian Primavera Pie

Pie crust pastry for 10-inch double
   crust pie
3 6-oz jars marinated artichoke hearts
5 green onions, finely chopped
1 Tbsp olive oil
1 lb ricotta cheese

1/2 cup sour cream
4 eggs, beaten
3/4 cup Parmesan cheese, grated
1 cup Swiss cheese, shredded
1/2 tsp tarragon
1/2 tsp salt
Egg yolk

Divide pastry in half and roll out dough 1/8-inch thick; line a 10-inch pie pan.

Drain artichoke hearts and cut in halves.

Sauté onions in olive oil until tender.

In a bowl beat together ricotta cheese, sour cream, eggs, Parmesan cheese, Swiss cheese, tarragon, and salt. Stir in artichoke hearts and onions.

Pour filling into pastry shell. Roll out remaining dough and cover pie. Turn under edges of pastry and flute. Prick crust with a fork and brush with egg yolk mixed with 1 Tbsp water.

Bake in a preheated 400 degree oven for 40 minutes until crust is golden.

6 chicken breast halves
1 lb lean fresh pork
1 lb fresh salt pork
1 chicken liver
1/2 tsp salt
1/4 tsp pepper
3 Tbsp brandy
1½ recipes for pie crust pastry
3 strips bacon
Egg yolk, beaten

Bone and skin chicken breasts. Reserve 3 breast halves and cut into filets. Grind remaining chicken with fresh pork, salt pork, and chicken liver. Season with salt, pepper, and brandy.

Roll out pastry 1/4-inch thick. Use 3/4 of dough to line a buttered hinged, or loaf style, pâté mold—allowing 1-inch of the pastry to extend beyond the rim. Press dough firmly into corners of mold. Lay 2 strips of bacon in the bottom. Cover with 1/3 of the ground chicken-meat mixture. Place a layer of chicken filets on top and cover with another 1/3 of the ground meat mixture, packing ingredients in well. Cover with remaining chicken filets and ground meat mixture, then top with a strip of bacon.

Fold edges of bottom crust inward over filling. Cut remaining dough to fit over top of pâté. Moisten edges and place over filling, pressing firmly down around inside rim. Seal edges of pastry with a fork or crimper. Decorate with pastry cut-outs. Prick crust several places. Cut a small hole in center of crust and insert a tiny foil funnel to allow space for fat to rise and be contained during baking.

Brush crust with egg yolk and bake in a preheated 350 degree oven for 1 1/2 hours. Cool pâté before unmolding.

1 lb round steak, finely diced
1 cup raw potatoes, finely diced
1 cup onions, finely chopped
1/2 tsp thyme
1 tsp salt
1/4 tsp ground black pepper
1 recipe for pie crust pastry
6 Tbsp butter
6 Tbsp parsley, chopped
Egg yolk, beaten
1/2 cup heavy cream

In a bowl combine diced round steak, potatoes and onions. Season with thyme, salt, and pepper.

Roll out pie crust pastry 1/8-inch thick and cut into 5-inch circles.

Spoon 3 Tbsp of filling on one side of each circle. Dot with 1 Tbsp of butter and sprinkle with 1 Tbsp of parsley. Moisten edges of pastry and fold over into turnovers. Crimp dough together with a fork. Prick top, and brush with egg yolk mixed with 1 Tbsp water.

Bake in a preheated 325 degree oven for 1 hour; 15 minutes before pasties are done, make a small hole in the top of the crust and spoon 2 Tbsp of heavy cream into the hole. (If crust browns too quickly during baking, cover turnovers with foil.)

1 package hot roll mix
1/4 cup warm water
1/2 cup hot milk
1/4 cup sugar
1/4 tsp salt
1/4 cup butter
1/2 tsp lemon peel, grated
1 egg, beaten
8-oz container small curd cottage cheese

1 egg yolk, beaten
1/4 cup sugar
1/2 tsp lemon peel, grated
1 Tbsp soft butter
1/4 tsp salt
1/2 cup chopped raisins
1 egg white
2 Tbsp sugar
1/2 tsp cinnamon

Dissolve yeast from hot roll mix in warm water. Combine milk, sugar, salt, butter and lemon peel in a bowl; cool until lukewarm. Stir in egg and yeast. Add flour from hot roll mix and blend well. Cover dough and let rise until it has doubled in size in about 1 1/2 hours. Punch down dough and knead four or five times. Roll out dough into a 15-inch square, and leave for 5 minutes. Cut into individual 2 1/2-inch squares.

In a bowl combine cottage cheese, egg, sugar, lemon peel, salt, butter and raisins.

Spoon 1 rounded tsp of cottage cheese filling on center of each square of dough; fold over dough pinching edges together tightly.

Place rolls, seam side down, in a buttered baking dish. Cover and let dough rise until rolls have doubled in size in about 45 minutes. Brush top of rolls with egg white and dust with sugar mixed with cinnamon. Bake in a preheated 375 degree oven for 30 minutes or until rolls are golden brown.

1 clove garlic, minced
1/2 cup green onions, minced
2 Tbsp butter
1/2 lb ground round
1 tomato, peeled and chopped
1 tsp salt
1 Tbsp curry powder
1/8 tsp red pepper
1 Tbsp parsley, chopped
1 3/4 cup all purpose flour
1 tsp salt
3 Tbsp butter, melted
1/3 cup yogurt ,
1 1/2 pt peanut oil

Sauté garlic and green onions in butter for 5 minutes. Add meat and cook until brown. crumbling meat with a fork. Stir in tomato, salt, curry powder, red pepper and parsley. Simmer for 5 minutes. Drain meat mixture and cool.

Sift flour and salt into a bowl and stir in butter and yogurt. Knead dough until smooth; cover and let stand 30 minutes. Roll out dough 1/8-inch thick on a floured board and cut into 4-inch squares.

Spoon 1 Tbsp of meat filling on each square and fold over into a triangle. Moisten edges of dough with water and seal tightly together. Heat oil until very hot, and deep fry turnovers, a few at a time, until golden brown. Drain on paper towel before serving.

1 package Hot Roll Mix
1/2 cup Parmesan cheese, grated
3 onions, peeled and cut in rings
4 Tbsp olive oil
6 ripe tomatoes, peeled and diced
1/4 cup pitted black olives, sliced
1/2 clove garlic, minced
1/2 tsp oregano
1/2 tsp rosemary
1 tsp salt
1/4 tsp black pepper
2-oz can anchovy fillets
6 pimiento-stuffed green olives, sliced
1 Tbsp olive oil

Prepare basic Hot Roll Mix by dissolving the yeast in warm water and blending it thoroughly with the dry ingredients. Divide dough in half. You need only half of this dough to make the Pissaladiere; refrigerate the other half for future use.

Roll out dough 1/4-inch thick and line a greased pizza pan. Crimp dough around edges. Sprinkle bottom of shell with Parmesan cheese.

Sauté onions in 2 Tbsp olive oil until tender. Cool and spoon over cheese.

Heat 2 more Tbsp of olive oil in a skillet and add tomatoes, olives, garlic, oregano, rosemary, salt, and pepper. Simmer for 15 minutes until the tomatoes have the consistency of a lumpy sauce. Spoon tomato sauce over onions.

Bake in a preheated 400 degree oven for 25 minutes.

Arrange anchovies over top of Pissaladiere, lattice fashion, to form diamond patterns. Place a slice of stuffed olive in the center of each diamond. Brush with olive oil before serving.

*In France Pissaladiere is made with homemade yeast dough; but we recommend Hot Roll Mix as a quick and easy substitute.

1 recipe for puff pastry
3/4 cup butter
2/3 cup flour
1 qt milk, warm
6 egg yolks, beaten
1 lb Swiss cheese, grated
1 tsp salt
1/4 tsp black pepper

Roll out puff pastry 1/8-inch thick, and cut in 3 strips 4 x 12-inches. Place strips on a greased baking sheet, and bake in a preheated 450 degree oven for 10 minutes; reduce temperature to 350, and continue baking until pastry is puffed and golden brown.

Melt butter in a skillet and slowly stir in flour. Gradually add warm milk and cook until sauce thickens. Add a little white sauce to beaten eggs and slowly stir eggs back into sauce. Stir in 3/4 of the Swiss cheese and season with salt & pepper. Cook for a few minutes until sauce is smooth.

Place 1 strip of puff pastry in the bottom of a rectangular pan and spoon 1/3 of cheese sauce over the top. Place a second strip over first strip of pastry in the pan, and cover with more sauce. Top with remaining pastry strip and sauce. Sprinkle with 1/4 of the Swiss cheese, and bake in a preheated 450 degree oven for 5 minutes.

4 green onions, fincly chopped
1/3 lb fresh mushrooms, sliced
2 Tbsp butter
4 cups cooked chicken, skinned & diced
1/2 tsp salt
1/4 tsp pepper
2 Tbsp parsley, chopped
1/2 tsp tarragon
2 eggs, beaten
1 1/2 cups Swiss cheese, shredded
16 sheets filo pastry (see page 13
   for preparation of filo pastry.)
1/2 cup butter, melted

Garnish: sour cream

Sauté onions and mushrooms in butter until tender.

In a bowl combine onions, mushrooms, chicken, salt, pepper, parsley, and tarragon. Stir in eggs and cheese.

Lay out 1 sheet of filo pastry and brush with melted butter. (Filo pastry is almost a duplicate of strudel pastry and makes a convenient substitute.) Place another sheet of filo pastry on top of the first and brush with butter.

Spoon 2/3 of a cup of chicken filling along one end of the rectangle, leaving a margin of 2-inches in from the end as well as both sides. Fold in both ends and loosely roll up the strudel. Brush with butter, and place on a greased baking sheet. Repeat this process until filling is used up.

Bake in a 400 degree oven for 25 minutes, or until crust is golden brown. Garnish with sour cream. Each strudel serves 1 person.   •

1/2 lb ground round
1/2 lb ground pork
1 onion, finely chopped
2 Tbsp salad oil
1 tsp salt
1 clove garlic, minced
1/4 tsp cinnamon
1/4 tsp pepper
1/4 tsp ground cloves

1/2 cup beef stock
4 Tbsp tomato paste
2 Tbsp red vinegar
1 tsp sugar
3 Tbsp currants
1/4 cup black olives, chopped
2 hard-cooked eggs, chopped
1 recipe for pie crust pastry
Egg yolk, beaten

Brown beef, pork, and onions in a skillet with salad oil, crumbling meat with a fork. Add salt, garlic, cinnamon, pepper, cloves, beef stock, tomato paste, vinegar, sugar, and currants. Simmer until liquid reduces to about 1/4 cup. Stir in black olives and eggs.

Roll out pie crust pastry 1/8-inch thick, and cut into 5-inch rounds.

Spoon 3 Tbsp of filling on half of each round. Moisten edges of pastry, fold over empanadas and seal edges together with a fork Brush with egg yolk mixed with 1 Tbsp water.

Bake in a 425 degree oven for 20 minutes, or until crust is golden brown.

These Slavic turnovers are tradition-ally made with the following sour cream pastry, and stuffed with meat or cab-bage filling.

Sour Cream Pastry

1/4 lb butter
2 cups sifted all purpose flour
1 egg yolk
1/2 tsp salt
4 Tbsp water
5 Tbsp sour cream

Crumble butter and flour together with your fingertips until butter is evenly distributed in tiny balls. Stir in egg yolk mixed with salt and water. Add sour cream and knead dough until

it is smooth. Form into a ball, wrap in wax paper and chill 1 1/2 hours.

Roll out pastry 1/8-inch thick and cut into 3-inch circles.

Spoon 1 Tbsp of filling on each round; moisten edges of dough and fold over, sealing edges together with a fork. Brush piroshki with beaten egg mixed with 1 Tbsp water, and prick crust with fork.

Bake in a preheated 350 degree oven for 25 minutes, or until browned.

Meat Filling

1 onion, minced
2 Tbsp butter
1 lb cooked beef, ground
1/2 tsp salt
1/4 tsp nutmeg

1/4 tsp pepper
2 hard-cooked eggs, finely chopped
1 slice white bread soaked in milk
1 Tbsp parsley, chopped
Beef stock

Sauté onions in butter until tender. Add cooked beef, salt, nutmeg, pepper, and eggs.

Squeeze milk from bread slice and crumble bread into mixture. Add parsley and sufficient beef stock to moisten filling.

Ukrainian Cabbage Filling

1/2 head of cabbage, shredded
1 large onion, finely chopped
5 Tbsp butter
2 hard-cooked eggs, chopped
1 tsp salt
1/2 tsp sugar
1 Tbsp fresh dill, or dill weed

Blanch cabbage in boiling water 1 minute. Drain and rinse with cold water. Squeeze cabbage carefully to eliminate all water.

Sauté onions in butter for a few minutes, and add cabbage. Simmer vegetables for 20 minutes. stirring frequently until cabbage is soft, but not browned.

Combine vegetables with eggs and season with salt, sugar, and dill. Cool filling before using.

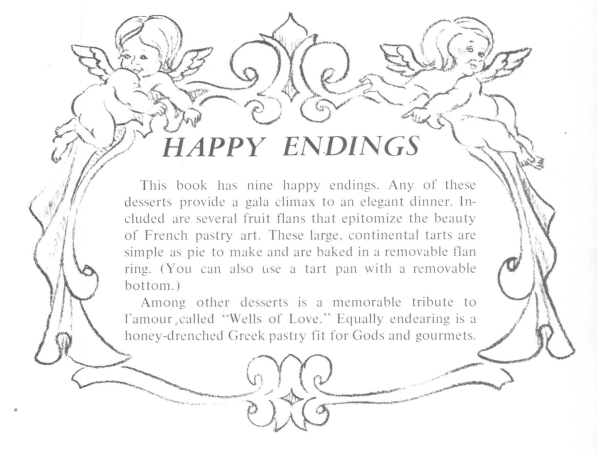

HAPPY ENDINGS

This book has nine happy endings. Any of these desserts provide a gala climax to an elegant dinner. Included are several fruit flans that epitomize the beauty of French pastry art. These large, continental tarts are simple as pie to make and are baked in a removable flan ring. (You can also use a tart pan with a removable bottom.)

Among other desserts is a memorable tribute to l'amour called "Wells of Love." Equally endearing is a honey-drenched Greek pastry fit for Gods and gourmets.

Fresh Fruit Flan

1 tsp vanilla
1 cup heavy cream, whipped
9-inch baked flan shell made with sweet
    pie pastry
1 lb ripe peaches or pears, peeled and
    sliced
1/4 cup apricot jam
2 Tbsp water

Garnish: toasted, almond slivers

Blend vanilla with whipped cream, and spoon into a baked flan shell. Arrange fruit in overlapping, concentric circles on top of whipped cream.

Heat apricot jam with water until it melts into a syrup consistency. Strain and cool. Brush apricot glaze over top of fruit. Garnish with almond slivers.

1 1/4 cups all-purpose flour
1/4 tsp salt
1/2 tsp cinnamon
1/2 tsp powdered cloves
1 Tbsp cocoa
1 cup butter, softened
1 cup unblanched almonds, ground
1 tsp lemon rind, grated
2 egg yolks, beaten
1/2 cup sugar
1 1/2 cups raspberry jam
1 egg white
Confectioners' sugar

Sift together flour, salt, cinnamon, cloves, and cocoa. Add butter, and cut into flour with a pastry blender, or two knives. Add ground almonds and lemon rind then blend well. Combine egg yolks and sugar and stir into flour. Knead dough until smooth. Wrap in wax paper and chill 1 hour.

Roll out dough 1/8-inch thick between sheets of waxed paper. Press 2/3 of the dough into a 9-inch pie pan. Turn under the edges and crimp.

Spoon raspberry jam over the bottom of pastry.

Cut remaining dough into 1/2-inch strips; arrange strips in a lattice pattern over the top of jam. Seal strips to the sides of the pan by pressing lightly.

Beat egg white until foamy and brush over the top of the torte.

Bake in a 350 degree oven for 40 minutes, or until pastry is browned. Cool. Dust with confectioners' sugar.

3/4 cup crushed pineapple, drained
1 cup pineapple juice
1/2 cup sugar
1/8 tsp salt
3 large egg yolks, well beaten
3 egg whites
1/2 tsp vanilla
9-inch baked flan shell made with sweet
   pie pastry
3/4 cup heavy cream, whipped
1 Tbsp sugar

Drain pineapple and reserve juice. If necessary, add sufficient pineapple juice to make 1 cup.

Combine pineapple juice, sugar, and salt in top of a double boiler, and simmer for 10 minutes. Add a little of the hot syrup to egg yolks, and gradually stir eggs back into syrup. Cook custard until it thickens. Cool

Beat egg whites until stiff and fold into custard. Stir in vanilla.

Spoon drained pineapple over bottom of baked flan shell; pour custard over top. Chill.

Blend whipped cream with sugar and spread over top of flan.

1 10-oz package frozen raspberries,
   thawed
3 Tbsp brandy
1 pint vanilla ice cream, softened
1 cup heavy cream, whipped
6 puff pastry shells or cream puff shells

Garnish: whole fresh raspberries

Drain raspberries; then stir berries and brandy into softened ice cream. Fold in whipped cream.

Spoon into puff pastry shells or cream puff shells. Garnish with fresh berries.

(The ice cream may be softened to just the right consistency by keeping it in the bottom section of your refrigerator for an hour.)

3 cups plain applesauce
1/2 cup sugar
3 Tbsp brandy
1/2 tsp cinnamon
1 lemon rind, grated
2 Tbsp butter
9-inch partially baked flan shell made
    with sweet pie pastry
3 apples, cored and peeled
3 Tbsp sugar
1/3 cup apricot jam
2 Tbsp water

Garnish: whipped cream

Put applesauce in a saucepan together with sugar, brandy, cinnamon, and lemon rind. Simmer until applesauce cooks down and thickens. Stir in butter.

Spoon applesauce into partially baked flan shell.

Cut apples into thin lengthwise slices, and lay apple slices over top of flan in overlapping, concentric circles. Dust with sugar.

Bake 30 minutes in a 350 degree preheated oven. Unmold flan onto serving dish.

Heat apricot jam with water until it melts into a syrup consistency. Strain glaze and slightly cool. Brush top of flan with apricot glaze. Serve with whipped cream.

Pie crust pastry for 9-inch single crust pie
1/3 cup black walnuts, ground
1 Tbsp sugar
11 oz cream cheese, softened

2 large eggs, beaten
1 tsp vanilla
1 cup sugar
1 cup sour cream

Prepare pie crust pastry and blend in black walnuts and sugar. Roll out pastry and line a 9-inch tart pan.

In a bowl, beat softened cream cheese and gradually add eggs, vanilla, and 1/2 cup sugar. Stir until mixture is smooth.

Pour into pie shell and bake in a 350 degree oven for 25 minutes. Reduce heat to 275, and continue baking another 5 minutes. Cool.

Combine remaining 1/2 cup of sugar with sour cream, and spread over pie.

Greek Baklava

1 lb butter, melted, kept hot
1 lb filo sheets
2 lbs walnuts, shelled, peeled and
    finely chopped
1 tsp cinnamon
1 tsp ground cloves
1 1/2 lb jar honey

Butter a shallow pan 10 x 14 x 2 inches. Place 1 sheet of filo pastry on the bottom, and turn under the edges to fit the pan. Brush pastry with melted butter. Place a second sheet of pastry over the first, folding under the edges. Brush with butter. Cover with a third and fourth sheet of pastry, brushing each sheet with butter.

Spoon 1/2 cup of walnuts over top of fourth sheet, and sprinkle with a little cinnamon and cloves. Cover with an additional 4 sheets of individually buttered pastry sheets. Sprinkle with 1/2 cup of walnuts, and dust with more cinnamon and cloves.

Repeat process until only 4 sheets of pastry remain. Butter remaining sheets and place over top of Baklava. Cut Baklava into diamond shaped pieces with a sharp knife.

Bake in a 350 degree oven for 30 minutes or until top is crisp and brown. Remove from oven and pour honey over the entire surface of the hot Baklava. Cool.

Cover pan with waxed paper and let Baklava stand for 24 hours before serving so the honey will be absorbed into the pastry.

Chocolate Chestnut Tarts

2 oz unsweetened chocolate
4 Tbsp butter, softened
1 cup French glacé creme chestnuts
2 tsp vanilla
1/3 cup heavy cream, whipped
6 baked 3-inch tart shells made with
   sweet pie pastry

Garnish: slivered bitter chocolate

Melt chocolate in a double boiler over hot water.

Blend butter with glace creme chestnuts and stir in chocolate and vanilla. Fold in whipped cream.

Spoon into baked tart shells and garnish with slivers of bitter chocolate.

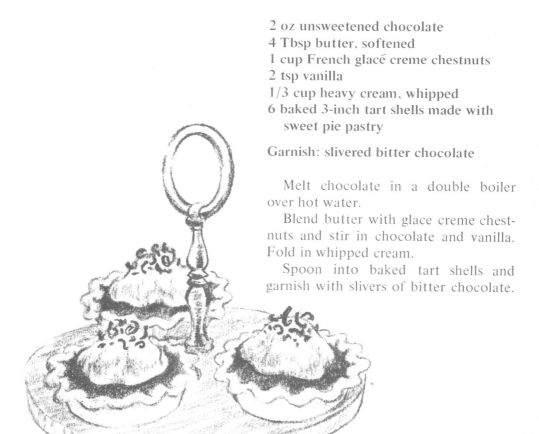

2 medium-size oranges
1/4 cup sugar
Juice of 1/2 lemon
2/3 cup water
1 cup sugar
2 1/2 Tbsp cornstarch
1/4 cup butter, softened
3 eggs
2 Tbsp Cointreau
Pie crust pastry for 9-inch double crust
Egg yolk
1 cup heavy cream, whipped
2 Tbsp confectioners' sugar
2 tsp orange rind, chopped

Wash oranges, remove orange surface of rind and chop finely. Separate oranges into sections and put into a saucepan; squeeze out juice from oranges leaving sections in pan. Add orange rind, 1/4 cup sugar, lemon juice, and water. Bring to a boil and gently simmer, uncovered, for 15 minutes. Cool.

Mix 1 cup sugar and cornstarch in a bowl. Stir in butter, and gradually beat in eggs. Stir in marmalade mixture and Cointreau.

Roll out 1/2 of the pastry to 1/8-inch thickness and line pie pan.

Pour in marmalade filling.

Roll out remaining dough and cut into 1/2-inch strips. Arrange strips in a lattice pattern over top of pie, sealing the ends of the strips to the edge of pie. Brush with egg yolk mixed with 1 Tbsp water.

Bake in a preheated 425 degree oven for 10 minutes; reduce to 350 degrees, and continue baking another 30 minutes, or until pie is set.

Garnish with whipped cream mixed with powdered sugar and orange rind.

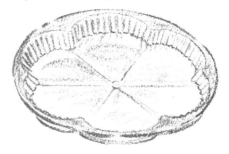

Index